Succulents

A Field Guide

PHILADELPHIA

RP Minis®
Hachette Book Group
1290 Avenue of the Americas, New York, NY 10104
www.runningpress.com
@Running_Press

First Edition: April 2022

Published by RP Minis, an imprint of Perseus Books, LLC, a subsidiary of Hachette Book Group, Inc. The RP Minis name and logo is a registered trademark of the Hachette Book Group.

ISBN: 978-0-7624-7916-0

CONTENTS

Introduction

Welcome to the singular, spectacular, and occasionally spiky world of succulents. You've probably at least heard of these exotic-looking plants, which have become increasingly ubiquitous in hipster windowsills and on the 'gram of lifestyle influencers. But what are succulents, why do they have such a savory-sounding name, and why are they so popular?

This book is designed to plant seeds of appreciation for these perfect little plants and to help you gain a better understanding for succulents. Learn what they are, what makes them so great, and discover some of the most popular types and varieties. Then find instructions for how to compose your own everlasting, maintenance-free succulents using the items included in this kit.

Let's get growing—er, going!

What Are Succulents?

Think of succulents as the camels of the plant world. Basically they're plants that excel at preserving water in structures like leaves and stems.

This A+ ability to retain water means that succulents are able to withstand exceedingly dry and sunny settings for prolonged periods of time. In fact they thrive in arid environments like deserts, but many also do well in less extreme settings, such as sunny windowsills.

To be clear, a succulent doesn't refer to a specific type of plant. Rather, it includes a variety of different plants with moisture-preserving powers. According to some estimates, there are over 10,000 succulent varieties.

So why the savory-sounding name? The word *succulent* derives from the Latin *sucus*, meaning "juice" or "sap," and in the case of succulent plants, this refers to the moisture they store inside.

Scintillating Succulents

Succulents have become the pop stars of the plant world. They're extremely low-maintenance and they're cute. Also, succulents don't need a lot. Many prefer high sun and detest extreme cold, but otherwise they mostly thrive on willful neglect. Some can even survive for weeks on end without water.

Yet despite the apparent lack of care required, they exude an effortless cool. Their unusual and sometimes alien-like appearance helps them make a statement in any room. Succulents aren't just easy on the eyes—they're quirky little characters, too. Here are a few things you might not know about these popular plants:

- Many succulents are green (duh). But the plant palette doesn't stop there. You can find succulents in just about any color of the rainbow, from flaming red to blush pink to vibrant orange and beyond.

- Succulents come in all shapes and sizes. Talk about extremes! The tiniest of succulents might measure in at only an inch or two. On the flip side, one of the largest succulents you'll find is the Baobab tree of Africa, which can grow as high as an eight-story building!

- Some succulents, like aloe vera, are highly valued for their medicinal qualities. Applying a little aloe to sunburn or razor burn can help speed up the healing process. Plant power, indeed!

- Succulents can make you smarter. Just looking at flora (even in photographic form) can enhance memory. So yes—the faux succulents in this kit could be good for your brain.

Scouting Succulents

Curious about some of the different types of succulents out there? Here are some of the most popular types:

- **Aloe:** There are many aloe succulents, but the most popular is aloe vera, which is characterized by thick green leaves with a pointed shape, soft texture, and variegated white spots. Aloe vera is used for medicinal purposes, in food and beverage, and in beauty products.

- **Crassula:** There's quite a variety of crassula succulents. Some are ground covers, others love cascading from baskets, and still others are capable of growing into six-foot shrubs. One of the most popular is *crassula ovata* or jade plant, a succulent shrub with thick, rounded leaves and a sturdy trunk.

- **Gasteria:** With thick, tongue-shaped leaves, gasteria succulents are often confused for aloes. The difference? Gasteria have unusual stomach-shaped flowers. One of the most popular varieties is *gasteria maculata*, a.k.a. Little Warty—a succulent with thick green leaves dotted with small white bumps.

- **Kalanchoe:** Prominent blooms are the first thing you'll notice with kalanchoe succulents. One of the most popular varieties is *kalanchoe blossfeldiana*, commonly called Flaming Katy, and featuring large, vibrant flowers that bloom in the spring.

- **Sempervivum:** Despite their ornate, complicated-looking rosette formations, sempervivum succulents, also known as hens and chicks, are actually among the easiest to take care of. In fact, the name *sempervivum* translates as "live forever." They can tolerate both extreme cold and extreme drought conditions.

Succulent Success

Got more of a black thumb than a green thumb? Great news: the succulents in this kit are guaranteed to succeed in any setting. Enjoy the lovely look of exotic succulents as a fridge adornment that comes together in mere minutes.

YOU'LL NEED:

- Kit contents (3 corks with pre-drilled holes, 3 faux succulents, magnets with adhesive backing)
- Glue (hot glue gun or heavy-duty craft glue)
- Optional: small portions of soil

Step 1: If using soil, gently place it on the top (drilled side) of the cork. Place a tiny dab of glue on the stem of a succulent, and immediately place it in the pre-drilled hole. Let the glue dry completely before moving on to the next step.

Step 2: Apply the adhesive magnets by removing the peel and adhering the sticky side to the back of the cork.

Voila! The easiest succulents you'll ever take care of!

This book has been bound using handcraft methods
and Smyth-sewn to ensure durability.

Illustration credits:
Book Cover & p 1 © ElenaMevedeva/Getty Images,
Box & pp 2–3, 14, 17, 21: Homunkulu28/Getty Images,
pp 6–7: negoworks/Getty Images,
pp 10–11: annaveroniq/Getty Images,
p 18: tukkata/Getty Images,
p 23: lamnee/Getty Images,
Box & p 26, 30–31: Yuliya Derbisheva/Getty Images

Designed by **Josh McDonnell**

Written by **Jessie Oleson Moore**